ESSENTIAL LIBRARY OF SOCIAL CHANGE

# CIVIL RIGHTS MOVEMENT

**ABDO**
Publishing Company

ESSENTIAL LIBRARY OF SOCIAL CHANGE

# CIVIL RIGHTS MOVEMENT

## by Michael Capek

**Content Consultant**

Steven F. Lawson
Professor Emeritus of History
Rutgers University

# CREDITS

Published by ABDO Publishing Company, PO Box 398166, Minneapolis, MN 55439. Copyright © 2014 by Abdo Consulting Group, Inc. International copyrights reserved in all countries. No part of this book may be reproduced in any form without written permission from the publisher. The Essential Library™ is a trademark and logo of ABDO Publishing Company.

Printed in the United States of America,
North Mankato, Minnesota
052013
092013

 THIS BOOK CONTAINS AT LEAST 10% RECYCLED MATERIALS.

Editor: Rebecca Felix
Series Designer: Emily Love

Photo credits: Bill Hudson/AP Images, cover, 2; Don Cravens/Time & Life Pictures/Getty Images, 6, 11, 14; Jupiter Images/Comstock/Thinkstock, 16; Russell Lee/Library of Congress, 20; AP Images, 25, 26, 32, 38, 42, 53, 60, 62, 69, 73, 81, 83; Carl Iwasaki/Time & Life Pictures/Getty Images, 28; Francis Miller/Time & Life Pictures/Getty Images, 36, 54; Bob Jordan/AP Images, 40; Horace Cort/AP Images, 45, 66, 74; Michael Ochs Archives/Getty Images, 49; John Duprey/NY Daily News Archive via Getty Images, 65; Hulton Archive/Getty Images, 76; Charles Kelly/AP Images, 85; Robert Abbott Sengstacke/Getty Images, 88; Spencer Grant/Getty Images, 93; Charles Rex Arbogast/AP Images, 97; Red Line Editorial, 100, 101

Library of Congress Control Number: 2013932966

## Cataloging-in-Publication Data

Capek, Michael.
Civil rights movement / Michael Capek.
p. cm. -- (Essential library of social change)
Includes bibliographical references and index.
ISBN 978-1-61783-885-9
1. Civil rights movements--United States--History--20th century--Juvenile literature. 2. African Americans--Civil rights--Juvenile literature. 3. United States--Race relations--Juvenile literature. I. Title.
323/.0973--dc23

2013932966

# CONTENTS

## CHAPTER 1

# THE MONTGOMERY BUS BOYCOTT

**A**s usual, the Cleveland Avenue bus in Montgomery, Alabama, was crowded the night of December 1, 1955. It was evening rush hour, and people all over town, black and white, hurried to climb aboard. Among them was Rosa Parks, a middle-aged seamstress and longtime resident of Montgomery. Parks was also a respected member of the black community and belonged to the National Association for the Advancement of Colored People (NAACP). As she boarded the bus that night, Parks paid her fare along with everyone else. Then she looked for a place to sit at the rear of the bus.

Parks was well aware that as an African American, she was required by law to ride in the back seats. The front ten rows were reserved for white people only. Segregation had been a social reality throughout the South for more than a century. Parks knew white people and black people did not sit, worship, play, go to school, eat, work, or do anything else together.

Most of the back bus seats were filled already, so Parks took a seat farther forward. She sat just behind the section for whites only, but next to several other black passengers. The bus moved on and more people boarded at each stop. Soon, the first ten rows were filled.

The bus driver noticed white passengers were standing in the aisles while black passengers remained seated. He shouted for Parks and the other black passengers to stand, even though they were not sitting in the whites-only section. Three black passengers rose and went to stand in the aisle at the rear of the bus, but Parks was not one of them.

The driver called out to her again and again. Parks heard him and understood what was expected of her. But she had made a decision. This day she would not give up her seat. And she was prepared for what would result: the bus driver summoned police officers, who boarded the bus and arrested her.

## A ONE-DAY PROTEST

Parks was not the first person of color in Montgomery to have her civil rights violated. There were many unjust laws at the time that denied black people their constitutional rights as US citizens. And many white authorities enforced these laws in an extreme or illegal way. Local black leaders had been waiting for a situation such as Parks's arrest to draw attention to illegal actions by city employees on city buses. They hoped to respond with a bold action. Black women made up the majority of bus passengers, especially those employed as maids and household workers. Local black leaders decided the arrest of a respected black woman provided the perfect opportunity for a dramatic demonstration.

Word spread through the black community to protest Parks's arrest by boycotting Montgomery's city buses for one day. Two young African-American ministers became leaders of the protest: the Reverend Ralph Abernathy and Doctor Martin Luther King Jr. Though men held leadership positions, black women, including Parks, also played a significant role in the subsequent boycott.

Jo Ann Robinson, a professor at Alabama State College, did much of the planning and organizational work behind the Montgomery bus boycott. Robinson was president of the Women's Political Council (WPC), an active and energetic group of mainly professional black women in Montgomery. Robinson and other WPC members had pressed city officials for years to change the way black passengers were treated on Montgomery's buses.

## MARTIN LUTHER KING JR.

The man who helped lead the Montgomery bus boycott also became a famous black civil rights leader. Martin Luther King Jr. was born in Atlanta, Georgia, to a strongly religious family. Black segregation and discrimination surrounded King throughout his upbringing. Growing up, he attended segregated but nurturing public schools. King went on to attend the distinguished, historically black institution Morehouse College in Atlanta. King then followed in his father's footsteps and became a pastor, where his talent for speaking was honed. He completed a doctorate in theology at Boston University after coming to Dexter Avenue Baptist Church in Montgomery as its pastor in 1954. When King joined the fight for civil rights, he gave life to the movement. His passion, ideals, and words united and gave hope to many. Nonviolent tactics and well-written speeches and prose by King greatly influenced the civil rights movement. King is honored as an American hero for his role in helping change history.

## BLACK CHURCHES

Religion played a strong role in the black civil rights movement. The local church was practically the only place black people were free to congregate and express themselves. During the civil rights movement, black people gathered in churches for moral support, information, and inspiration. Churches became social and political, as well as spiritual, centers. While some black churches preferred politics and the church remain separate, other black churches became very involved in the movement. It was logical that ministers from these supporting churches often assumed main leadership roles in protests and demonstrations. In fact, shortly after the Montgomery boycott, black ministers united to form the Southern Christian Leadership Conference (SCLC) with King as president. Their preaching and Christian faith formed the backbone of the black civil rights movement.

On December 5, fours days after Parks's arrest, dozens of buses were empty as 50,000 people—the entire black population of Montgomery— honored the boycott.[1] Thousands gathered in neighborhood churches for information and support. King, who was pastor at the Dexter Avenue Baptist Church, spoke before a huge audience gathered there. King was young and new to Montgomery. Many people had not met him yet or heard him speak. King talked about the goals of the protest, emphasizing that the boycott should

**Black citizens walked to and from work and other »
daily activities in Montgomery on February 1,
1956, months into the bus boycott.**

be thought of as the beginning of a larger battle for civil rights. His confidence and bold speaking style electrified the assembly, and soon his spirit and energy spread through the entire black community.

The boycott grew, and one day turned into weeks and months of Montgomery's black residents refusing to ride city buses. This was a tremendous sacrifice, as many had a difficult time getting to school or work without the buses. The boycott also affected the city. It lost thousands of dollars in bus fares every day. But city leaders refused to discuss making changes to the laws, so the black community remained steadfast in its boycott.

At first, boycott leaders demanded only that the city agree to treat black passengers equally to and as respectfully as white passengers. But as the protest continued, the black community determined that its goal should be getting the law changed to eliminate segregation on city buses.

## BROWDER V. GAYLE

Behind the scenes of the boycott, lawyers representing the NAACP began preparing a legal case. The case was not in defense of Parks, however. Though Parks's act ignited the boycott, lawyers concentrated on a similar situation that had occurred more quietly the April prior to Parks's arrest. Another African-American woman, Aurelia Browder, was arrested aboard a Montgomery bus after refusing to give up her seat to a white passenger. To avoid the public furor surrounding Parks's well-known situation, lawyers chose to push forward with Browder's case. NAACP lawyers filed a lawsuit on her behalf against Montgomery mayor W. A. Gayle, who oversaw city programs. The case attacked segregation on city buses directly, in hopes of completely ending seating arrangements based on race.

Despite the paralyzing boycott and the legal case, Montgomery city officials still refused to reconsider bus policies. After rounds of appeals, in November 1956, the Supreme Court ruled in *Browder v. Gayle* that segregated seating on Alabama city buses and trains was indeed illegal. It was ordered that all buses and trains in the state of Alabama be integrated immediately.

## THE NAACP LEGAL DEFENSE FUND

Thurgood Marshall was the lead NAACP attorney who prepared and presented the legal case of *Browder v. Gayle*. He was also the founder of the NAACP Legal Defense and Educational Fund (LDF), the legal arm of the NAACP. Over the next two decades, Marshall and the LDF became the legal engine that propelled the civil rights moment forward. Marshall later became the United States' first black Supreme Court justice.

Parks, *center*, sat among black and white passengers on a newly integrated Montgomery bus on December 26, 1956.

On December 21, 1957, after 13 months of boycotting, black citizens finally returned to Montgomery buses. Now they could sit in any seat they chose and did not have to give their seat up for anyone. Among the first to board that day were King and Abernathy. Photographs of that historic moment appeared in newspapers from coast to coast. Parks allowed her picture to be taken aboard a bus, too, but she was not particularly happy about it. She later wrote, "It didn't feel like a victory, actually. There still had to be a great deal to do."[2]

Parks was right. The victory in Alabama, while significant, did not end racial discrimination. Black people were still denied many rights. They were in for a long and difficult journey. ●

## CHAPTER 2

# RECONSTRUCTION AND OPPRESSION

**T**he black civil rights movement in the United States peaked during the period of violence, uprising, and change that occurred in the decades surrounding the 1960s. But injustice and discrimination against black Americans began with the slave trade in the 1600s, in which African people were forcibly brought to America as laborers. Slavery endured for more than 200 years. Its practice ended in 1865, after the American Civil

War (1861–1865), a bloody war between Northern and Southern states. Southern states wanted to break from the North over disagreements on many issues. Slavery was chief among them. Northern states fought to end slavery. Southern states fought to continue slavery. Many slaves worked and lived on plantations in the South, which produced crops such as cotton, rice, and tobacco and upheld the Southern economy.

Slavery was abolished at the war's end. The Thirteenth Amendment to the Constitution freed every slave. But ending a practice in place for more than two centuries proved difficult for the South. No longer able to rely on the free, forced labor of slavery, the South's economy was devastated. So was much of its land, which had seen many battles during the war. A period of reconstruction followed to protect newly freed African Americans and restore and unify the South.

During the Reconstruction Era, with the Fourteenth and Fifteenth Amendments, African Americans were granted citizenship, "equal protection of the laws," and the right to vote.[1] During a brief period of Reconstruction, while Northern troops were still in the South, black men took an active role in local, state, and federal governments. They filled such important positions as sheriffs, mayors,

## THE Ku Klux Klan

The KKK used intimidation, hate speech, and vandalism to oppress, scare, injure, and kill black people. Mobs of KKK members would attack, beat, torture, and then kill black people, often for no other reason than the color of their skin. This is called lynching. Because the members of the KKK wore white hooded sheets to conceal their identity, they were able to get away with these acts of terror without punishment. However, though membership was secret, it was well-known that many political and public officials belonged. The federal government fought back against the KKK by passing and enforcing legislation, known as the Force Acts, against its members in the early 1870s. This weakened the KKK. However, although the organization largely died out following the restoration of white Democratic governments in the South at the end of Reconstruction, it did not disappear. The KKK reemerged and was responsible for many crimes against blacks in the South throughout the civil rights movement.

commissioners of education, and district attorneys. They were elected to the US Senate and House of Representatives.

But a period of violence and fear also began in the years following the American Civil War. The terrorist group known as the Ku Klux Klan (KKK) formed. The KKK consisted of many groups of white supremacists in the South. Members' identities were kept secret. Also, the general public and government in the South openly engaged in another form of racial discrimination, known as Jim Crow, during this time. White supremacy was at the core of both the KKK and Jim Crow.

In 1896, the US Supreme Court legalized segregation in a case called *Plessy v. Ferguson*. The court ruled cities and states could legally force black people to use separate public facilities, including schools. Cities and states were to provide something considered equal in quality to the facilities white people used. But Southern states adopted segregation without providing for equality. In most places throughout the South, the designated black facilities were dirty and dreary, at best. Blacks were essentially treated as second-class citizens. Throughout the first decade of the 1900s, blacks were also disenfranchised, meaning their right to vote was taken away. States used literacy tests, complex registration procedures, and poll taxes to keep black men from registering and voting. By 1901, due to

## JIM CROW

The stifling system of laws and customs known as Jim Crow was named for a black-faced character made popular in a form of theater that acted out racial stereotypes in the late 1800s and early 1900s. The Jim Crow character was a clownish figure whose exaggerated gestures and speech mocked the stereotypical characteristics of black people. The message Jim Crow sent was that black people were inferior, and therefore belittling, segregating, and dehumanizing them was not wrong.

Signs separated "colored" water jugs and restrooms from "white" facilities in a streetcar station in 1939.

Jim Crow laws and rising disfranchisement and bigotry, no black representatives remained in Congress.

Southern states rewrote their constitutions in order to forcibly separate blacks from whites in every aspect of life—and even death. Signs in nearly every Southern town pointed out the blacks-only drinking fountains, hospitals, toilets, waiting rooms, and cemeteries. Any black person who dared enter or use a facility for a white person was likely to be attacked. And white attackers would almost always walk away without punishment.

## WARS AND THE GREAT MIGRATION

When World War I (1914–1918) broke out in Europe in 1914, war production in the United States kicked into high gear. Recruiters headed south, hoping to utilize the many black workers in need of jobs. Many black people in the South responded to the calls for workers in the North and West. A factory job in a Northern city paid much more on average than a person could make sharecropping in the South. Thousands left their homes to seek hope and prosperity in the North. This stimulated a movement, known as the Great Migration, that was already under way and continued after the war. This movement was one of the largest movements of people in US history. Many Northern industrial cities, which previously had small black populations, were suddenly flooded with new black residents.

The sudden influx of people and newly crowded conditions brought discomfort and disagreements between white and black neighbors. Adding to tensions, blacks were often willing to work for less money than whites, leading many whites to worry they would lose their jobs to black migrators. When the war ended in 1918 and veterans returned home looking for work, the problems

## THE RED SUMMER OF 1919

Resentment caused by black people crowding into areas and taking jobs previously reserved for white people boiled over in the summer of 1919. These tensions resulted in a wave of violent black lynchings that broke out after World War I ended. Many black people had believed their civil rights would improve at war's end, due to black soldiers' contributions to the war effort. The outbreak of violent lynchings created anger across the country, and black people fought back. The worst violence occurred in Chicago, Illinois, where rioting lasted for 13 days. When it was over, 15 white people and 23 black people had been killed and more than 500 people injured.[2] More than 1,000 black families lost their homes when white people burned them.[3] That summer became known as "Red Summer" in reference to the bloodshed from the many riots. Before then, many believed blacks were unwilling to oppose white prejudice. The confrontations that summer signaled a change in the black community.

only worsened. Tensions were highest during the summer of 1919. During this time, blacks and whites clashed openly in many cities across the country. There were riots, violence, arrests, and a general feeling of unrest.

As the economic collapse known as the Great Depression caused distress in the United States in the decade after 1929, President Franklin D. Roosevelt established a program to bring economic relief. Called the New Deal, it aided blacks as part of the general population through its welfare and jobs programs. Although the New Deal did not challenge segregation,

Roosevelt did appoint blacks to positions in his government. Roosevelt's wife, Eleanor, was very supportive of civil rights issues and pressured her husband to do more.

After years of unrest and discrimination, black leaders issued a direct challenge for the president to act. In June 1941, labor leader A. Philip Randolph established the March on Washington Movement, threatening to bring thousands of black protesters to the nation's capital to campaign for equality. To avoid this demonstration, President Roosevelt issued an executive order that allowed African Americans to work in government-supported construction projects and factories. Roosevelt also created the Fair Employment

## THE HARLEM RENAISSANCE

During the 1920s, black writers, artists, and musicians were part of what became known as the Harlem Renaissance, an outpouring of works that reflected the history and culture of African Americans. Centered in the Harlem neighborhood of New York City, these talented people publicized the vitality of African Americans in withstanding racism and challenged white America to remove the barriers to racial equality. Their combined creativity produced a bright hope that art and music might help break down racial barriers. The Harlem Renaissance produced some of America's finest novelists, performers, painters, and poets, including Langston Hughes, Zora Neale Hurston, and Claude McKay.

Practice Committee, the first federal agency to improve racial progress since Reconstruction and to publicize job discrimination and attempt to resolve it.

When the United States plunged into World War II (1939–1945) in 1941, black Americans benefitted once again from the sudden openings in the job market. Once war came, civil rights leaders proclaimed a "Double V" for victory at home over racism and victory abroad over totalitarianism. However, although millions of black Americans found work in plants and factories, racial discrimination continued worsening. And civil leaders continued pressing their demands for equality.

A major victory came through the US Supreme Court. Beginning in the 1920s, the NAACP had challenged the all-white Democratic primary system in the South. Because the Republican Party was weak in the region, the real elections for public office took place within Democratic primaries, which barred blacks from voting. In 1944, in the case of *Smith v. Allwright*, the Supreme Court ruled all-white Democratic Party primaries violated the Fifteenth Amendment by excluding African Americans. By 1947, the percentage of blacks registered to vote in the South jumped from less than 5 percent to 12 percent.[4]

The black migration from the South to the North during the war strengthened black political power. Black people in the North could vote, and they could affect the

**The Tuskegee Airmen flew important supply and service missions during World War II. However, the all-black squadron was still segregated from white troops.**

balance of power in close state and national elections. However, none of these changes did much to reduce racial tensions.

During the war, black men had been drafted into the military and had fought honorably. This created the expectation among black communities that black Americans would be recognized as equal citizens and gain full civil rights. But black units were not allowed to fight with white units in that war. In a poll taken at war's end,

In 1948, President Truman signed a bill proclaiming February 1 as National Freedom Day, in remembrance of the day the Thirteenth Amendment was signed.

75 percent of white Americans said they expected relations between black and white Americans to grow worse in coming years.[5] Jim Crow discrimination, particularly in the South, was more intense and widespread than it had ever been. As a result, yet another wave of black people left the South.

## POSTWAR YEARS

After World War II ended, President Harry S. Truman was eager to win the support of black voters in the North. In 1946, he formed a biracial Committee on Civil

Rights to examine racial bias and violence in the United States. In 1947, the committee issued "To Secure These Rights," an ambitious call to action for the government to pass stronger laws against lynching and continued discrimination against black voters, among other measures. President Truman made it clear he would take steps to follow the committee's recommendations if he was reelected.

As the election approached, President Truman felt intense pressure from Randolph and Congressman Adam Clayton Powell Jr. to fulfill his promises. At the same time, the former wartime alliance between the United States and the Soviet Union collapsed. The two countries engaged in a conflict of ideologies and power known as the Cold War. President Truman reinstated the draft. The president knew black men would no longer willingly serve in a segregated, discriminatory army. In July 1948, he issued two executive orders. The first officially desegregated the federal workforce, making blacks eligible for government jobs. The second order was the desegregation of the US armed forces. These actions were a strong stand for African American rights and marked a shift in US politics. ●

## CHAPTER 3

— — —

# SEGREGATION AND EDUCATION

n the 1950s, a series of events took place in an effort to end school segregation. In the fall of 1950, Oliver Brown went to enroll his eight-year-old daughter, Linda, in school for the coming school year. He brought her to a whites-only school that was a few minutes' walk from their home in Topeka, Kansas. Linda had been attending an all-black school, but to get there each day, she had to walk across dangerous railroad tracks and ride a run-down bus across town. Her father wanted her to go to the school that was located closer to their home. Linda and her father were disappointed when the principal there told them Linda could not attend because she was black. Linda's father joined a class action suit NAACP lawyers were developing that would attempt to force schools across the nation to accept students regardless of race.

In 1950, more than 2 million black children were forced to attend segregated schools.[1] Segregated all-black Morton High School in Prince Edward County, Virginia, was so overcrowded some students had classes on school buses or in tar-paper shacks. One student was so disgusted with the poor facilities she led a walkout of the entire student body to protest. That demonstration resulted in a lawsuit, which became part of the same class action case Brown joined.

## BROWN V. BOARD OF EDUCATION OF TOPEKA

NAACP lawyers had struggled for years to end policies based on the *Plessy v. Ferguson* "separate but equal" ruling of 1896.[2] Integrating schools was a first step in that direction. Previously, the NAACP won cases before the Supreme Court that required states to provide equal access to higher education even if it involved integration of state universities. The NAACP then moved on to elementary and secondary schools. Its lawyers combined five education suits from four states and Washington, DC, into one case, *Brown v. Board of Education of Topeka*. The case would challenge the constitutionality of racial segregation in public schools.

Thurgood Marshall, the lawyer who would represent the Montgomery bus boycott in future years, was lead attorney for the NAACP at the time. In June 1952, he and his colleagues presented their case before the US Supreme Court. After days of testimony and debate, the court adjourned. The justices deliberated on the decision for months. The case was argued three separate times. Finally, on May 17, 1954—two years after the hearings began—the court's unanimous decision in *Brown v. Board of Education of Topeka* overturned *Plessy v. Ferguson* and ruled against the segregation of black and white students in public schools.

White supremacists in the South were outraged. Many Southern governors and senators proclaimed their states would not support or obey the ruling.

Fights aiming to squash segregation in other areas increased during this time as well. It was just months after the *Brown v. Board of Education of Topeka* ruling that the black community took another stand with the Montgomery bus boycott. Then, in 1955, the Supreme

Court ruled in a follow-up decision to *Brown* that public schools must desegregate "with all deliberate speed."[3] However, this phrase was unfortunately imprecise and so encouraged the South to delay desegregating for as long as possible. Federal judges from the South heard the cases initiated by black people wanting to integrate, which only made the likelihood of swift change more complex.

"We conclude that, in the field of public education, the doctrine of 'separate but equal' has no place. Separate educational facilities are inherently unequal. Therefore, we hold that the plaintiffs and others similarly situated for whom the actions have been brought are, by reason of the segregation complained of, deprived of the equal protection of the laws guaranteed by the Fourteenth Amendment. This disposition makes unnecessary any discussion whether such segregation also violates the Due Process Clause of the Fourteenth Amendment."[4]

—*US Supreme Court Chief Justice Earl Warren, presenting the Brown v. Board of Education of Topeka decision on May 17, 1954*

## EMMETT TILL

In the summer of 1955, a grisly murder incited black youth to become more involved in the civil rights movement. Emmett Till was a fun-loving 14-year-old black boy from Chicago, Illinois, who was not above showing off. That summer, Emmett visited relatives in rural Mississippi, where social rules about how black males behaved were

**Emmett Till**

very different from those in the North. One day during his
visit, Emmett characteristically accepted a dare from some
boys he met outside a grocery store. Acting on the dare,
Emmett went inside the store and called out "'Bye, Baby"
to the owner's white wife as he left.[5] Several days later, on
August 28, the owner and another white man showed up
at the house where Emmett was staying and dragged the
terrified boy away into the night.

Emmett's battered body was found three days later in a nearby river. A heavy piece of metal was tied around his neck with barbed wire. When his body was taken home to Chicago, his mother opened the casket lid and demanded that everyone look. A picture of Emmett's mutilated body was published in a black magazine. Emmett's murderers were arrested, but despite overwhelming evidence and eyewitness testimonies from Emmett's uncle and other black witnesses, both men were found not guilty by an all-white Mississippi jury.

The murder and the result of the trial shaped the conscience of a whole generation of young Americans, black and white. Many civil rights leaders and activists have pinpointed that incident as the one that caused a generation to stand up and fight against blatant racial injustice.

## THE LITTLE ROCK NINE

The battle to desegregate schools continued, and many attempts were met by angry confrontations. Crowds of white people blocked roads and school doors and gathered in front of schools to confront black parents who tried to enroll their children. Black children who did enroll in white schools faced harassment and humiliation by white children. Even white teachers shouted vulgar words and vicious threats to black students and their families to fight integration.

Similar to many other Southern schools, the Little Rock, Arkansas, school board had delayed putting the court's *Brown* ruling into effect. Finally, in 1957, the board announced that a few black students would be allowed to attend Little Rock's Central High School. They soon became known as the "Little Rock Nine" in newspaper and television reports.

On September 4, nine black students showed up at school. The building was ringed by a screaming mob of people. Arkansas National Guard troops, who were supposedly there to protect the black students, held back the mob. But when the black students arrived, the National Guard soldiers turn them away with fixed bayonets, obeying an order by the governor. One black girl was separated from the others. She was surrounded by angry white protesters, who

## CHOOSING THE LITTLE ROCK NINE

Daisy Bates, president of the Arkansas NAACP, was given the difficult task of choosing the black students who would attend Central High School, and she coordinated their enrollment. She was threatened and attacked for her role in integrating the students. One night a rock was thrown through her window. Attached was a note that read, "Stone this time. Dynamite next."[6]

shouted at her and harassed her. Police and National Guard troops did nothing to help the girl, who managed to escape to safety with the help of a white sympathizer.

Weeks later, on Friday, September 20, the troops withdrew. A federal judge granted a request from NAACP lawyers to stop the governor from using National Guard troops to prevent the black students from entering the school. The following Monday, September 23, an angry mob formed outside the school yet again. Little Rock police took over and escorted the black students into the school through a side door, unnoticed by the rioters. The crowd grew more aggressive upon learning the students were inside, and so police removed the Little Rock Nine from the school by noon that day.

Reports of the Little Rock riot infuriated President Dwight D. Eisenhower. The next day, September 24, he ordered the Arkansas National Guard to return to protect and assist black students, not bar them from the school. He also ordered US Army troops to move into the city and take charge of the situation.

The federal soldiers cleared the streets around Central High School and established order. On September 25, they escorted the nine black students to school in armored vehicles fixed with machine guns. To ensure the black students were safe once inside, each was assigned a soldier who accompanied the student into the

Elizabeth Eckford, *front*, one of the Little Rock Nine, attempted to enter Little Rock High on September 4, 1957, among sneering white parents, students, and guards.

building and remained with the student throughout the day. A number of the school's white students and teachers stayed home that day, but not all. Some welcomed their new classmates and tried to help them get settled.

Still, the Little Rock Nine encountered numerous problems, especially once President Eisenhower removed federal troops in late September, leaving only the National

Guard to provide protection. The guardsmen came from Arkansas and were only slightly older than the high school students. They therefore shared many of the same racial attitudes. Even with the guardsmen's presence, the black students endured a constant barrage of physical and verbal abuse.

While Little Rock simmered with tension, Congress took one small, yet significant, step toward ending racial discrimination with the passage of the Civil Rights Act of 1957. The first such act since Reconstruction, the law was largely symbolic, essentially creating a commission to monitor violations of civil rights, particularly discrimination against black voters. But the act did accomplish one important thing. It made Civil Rights a division of the Justice Department, giving the department the power to legally charge cities and states that discriminated against people because of race.

The following spring, in May 1958, Ernest Green became the first black student to graduate from Central High School in Little Rock. The crowd at the ceremony that day was mostly white. The attendees applauded the other graduates but were totally silent when Green received his diploma. However, in addition to Green's family, there was at least one other person there who was proud of him that day: civil rights leader King, who attended the ceremony and sat with Green's parents.

The following school year, 1958–1959, the governor of Arkansas and the state legislature closed all four of Little Rock's schools rather than see them integrated. Instead, they proposed a plan to convert the public school system into a segregated private system funded by local taxes. NAACP lawyers filed litigation challenging the plan. One year later, the Supreme Court decided in the NAACP's favor by ordering that the schools reopen on an integrated basis.

But the civil rights battle for black students was far from over. Many white students in Arkansas left public schools and enrolled in private, all-white schools to avoid integration. And states and local school districts found ways to get around court decisions, meaning many schools throughout the South remained segregated. ●

## PUPIL PLACEMENT LAWS

One way schools kept black students out was through pupil placement laws. These laws, adopted by many states, allowed local school districts to bar black students from attending white schools on grounds supposedly other than race—intelligence levels, moral characteristics, or preserving the peace.

« **Ernest Green on his graduation day from Little Rock High**

## CHAPTER 4

# NEW TACTICS, SAME RESPONSE

O n February 1, 1960, four black students in
Greensboro, North Carolina, were refused service
at the lunch counter at a Woolworth's store.
They decided to sit quietly at the counter in protest. The
students came back the next day with more students and
staged another sit-in. The counter filled up and picketers
arrived outside carrying signs supporting the sit-in.

The students replaced the sit-ins with boycotts of the store, which hurt the business economically. After five months of boycotts, the store's owner agreed to begin serving black students. Inspired by the Greensboro Four, as they were soon called, people in towns all over the nation were soon staging peaceful demonstrations. Many of these were coordinated by the Student Nonviolent Coordinating Committee (SNCC). The term *sit-in* became a household phrase and a potent weapon in the fight for civil rights.

In the summer of 1961, the Congress of Racial Equality (CORE), a nonviolent, interracial civil rights organization, planned a bold protest in the South. Many black people there were still denied service in restaurants and made to use separate public facilities. Many buses were still segregated as well, despite the Supreme Court ruling that made segregation illegal on buses and railroads crossing interstate lines, including the dining and toilet facilities at the stations along the routes. To challenge this situation, hundreds of black and white youth were recruited to sit together in segregated sections of depots and on interstate buses through the South. They became known as Freedom Riders.

A Freedom Rider bus was set on fire near
Anniston, Alabama, in May 1961.

As expected, such bold actions infuriated officials and hate groups. Freedom Riders were arrested and viciously attacked. In many places, riders were dragged from buses and beaten with fists, lead pipes, bats, and bottles. At a stop near Anniston, Alabama, a firebomb was launched into a bus full of riders. The attackers barricaded its exits. State troopers arrived, causing the attacking mob to back away from the bus and allowing those inside to escape. Many riders were beaten as they escaped. The bus was destroyed. But the Freedom Riders, some of them in splints and bandages, continued their journeys. The SNCC joined CORE in recruiting wave after wave of students to join the rides. Before the end of the summer, more than 300 Freedom Riders were in Southern jails.[1] In response,

Attorney General Robert F. Kennedy, with the support of his brother President John F. Kennedy, ordered the Interstate Commerce Commission to ensure the desegregation of bus and rail stations in the South that year.

Racial violence and protests across the South continued in the following years. Of the Southern cities where racial discrimination still existed, Birmingham, Alabama, was one of the most segregated and racially violent in 1963. Forty percent of Birmingham's citizens were black, but the city was completely run by a tough, no-nonsense group of white segregationists.[2] The toughest of these was Commissioner of Public

## "BULL" CONNOR

Theophilus Eugene "Bull" Connor was a politician with a deep-seated prejudice against black people. He often conspired with the KKK. A former sportscaster in Birmingham, Connor also held a seat in the Alabama House of Representatives in 1934. He went on to serve as Birmingham's city commissioner for many years. His strong opinions in favor of segregation became well-known during his four terms as commissioner. Birmingham voted to replace the commissioner-run government system with a mayor and council in the fall of 1962. So Connor ran for mayor, but he lost the vote. The new mayor did not take office until the following spring, in late May 1963. During this time, Connor ran the town. He was largely responsible for the police brutality in Birmingham.

Safety Theophilus Eugene "Bull" Connor. His hatred for and brutal treatment of civil rights protesters made him infamous.

In the spring of 1963, Birmingham minister Fred Shuttlesworth invited King to Birmingham. King would help Shuttlesworth lead a demonstration against segregation and discrimination. Although gaining national fame as a civil rights orator, King had achieved much less success on the ground. He had participated in sit-in demonstrations in Atlanta in 1960 for which he was arrested. His arrest became an issue in the 1960 presidential election, and when he received support from Democratic presidential candidate John F. Kennedy, black voters helped make the difference in his defeating Republican candidate Richard M. Nixon. King had not directly participated in the Freedom Rides, but he did lend his support to the riders when they got to Montgomery and were threatened by raging mobs. The following year, King was invited to participate in demonstrations against a variety of segregationist practices in Albany, Georgia. This led to his arrest and ended in defeat for integration. To maintain his role as a national civil rights leader, King needed a victory.

King's ally as a member of the Southern Christian Leadership Conference (SCLC), Shuttlesworth provided King with a splendid opportunity in Birmingham.

**Reverend Ralph Abernathy, *front left*, and King, *front right*, led demonstrators toward the Birmingham courthouse on April 12, 1963.**

Shuttlesworth named the demonstration Project C. The *C* stood for "confrontation." Joining them was King's close friend and associate, Abernathy.

The goal of their demonstration was to integrate Birmingham's downtown area. The city had received orders from the US Justice Department to end segregation, but old Jim Crow restrictions were still in place downtown. Whites-only signs still barred black citizens from many public facilities.

The Birmingham movement consisted mostly of blacks , but a few whites in the city were willing to speak out in protest. King, Shuttlesworth, Abernathy, and many others were arrested during the early days of protesting in April 1963. After their arrest, a group of white ministers bought space in the local newspaper and printed a letter, calling for King to stop the Birmingham protest and give moderators in the city more time to work out a solution.

King wrote a letter of his own in response from his jail cell. In it he explained in detail what the protest was about. He said the civil rights movement's goal was nationwide freedom. He discussed the difference between just and unjust laws. He spoke of religion and destiny and the horrible impact Jim Crow had, especially on the psychological well-being of black children. He carefully outlined why he and others had to continue their fight. King smuggled his letter page by page to his lawyers. But it did not end up being published until months later and so did not affect the campaign in Birmingham. In the years since, however, King's "Letter from Birmingham Jail" is viewed as one of the great documents of the American civil rights movement, if not of human history.

## THE CHILDREN'S CRUSADE

With its leaders in jail, the Birmingham campaign stalled. Many local supporters did not want to get involved because if they were arrested, they could lose their jobs. Then a fiery young black minister working for the SCLC, James Bevel, suggested a plan. What if black children protested? They did not have jobs to lose and many were eager to join the movement. It was risky, of course. Nobody wanted to

**VOICES OF THE MOVEMENT**

An excerpt from Martin Luther King Jr.'s "Letter from Birmingham Jail," written on April 16, 1963:

"We know through painful experience that freedom is never voluntarily given by the oppressor; it must be demanded by the oppressed. . . . For years now I have heard the word 'Wait!' It rings in the ear of every Negro with piercing familiarity. This 'Wait' has almost always meant 'Never.' . . . Perhaps it is easy for those who have never felt the stinging darts of segregation to say, 'Wait.' But when you have seen vicious mobs lynch your mothers and fathers at will and drown your sisters and brothers at whim; when you have seen hate filled policemen curse, kick and even kill your black brothers and sisters; . . . when you are forever fighting a degenerating sense of 'nobodiness'—then you will understand why we find it difficult to wait. There comes a time when the cup of endurance runs over, and men are no longer willing to be plunged into the abyss of despair."[3]

put children in harm's way. And yet, Bevel felt televised images of children being arrested would have a powerful, emotional impact on the American public and would jump-start the protest.

By April 20, King, Shuttlesworth, and Abernathy had been released from jail, and they agreed that a "children's crusade" would make a dramatic statement.[4] On May 2, 1963, the first wave of more than 1,000 black children between the ages of six and 18 marched from the Sixteenth Street Baptist Church toward downtown Birmingham.[5] Police arrested hundreds of them almost immediately. Just then, another group appeared and behind them another and another. By the end of that first day, 959 children were in Birmingham jails.[6]

The next day, as hundreds of children again marched toward downtown Birmingham, fire trucks arrived and began shooting powerful streams of water at the small protesters. At a pressure strong enough to remove bark from a tree, the water slammed the children against curbs, cars, and buildings. Spectators watched, horrified, as small bodies were sent skidding and rolling across the pavement. Police then set dogs, trained to bring down violent criminals, on the children and adults who tried to help them.

Birmingham's black community was enraged by the brutality and rallied the next day. Many called for armed

**Children were battered by pressurized water during the May 1963 protest marches in Birmingham.**

warfare against Connor and his police force. King and Bevel pleaded for restraint on both sides. Day after day, protest marches continued. Each time, riot police met protesters with maximum force, sending many, including Shuttlesworth, to the hospital. Within only a few days,

> **"The water stung like a whip and hit like a cannon. . . . The force of it knocked you down. . . . We tried to hold onto the building, but that was no use."[8]**
>
> *— Carolyn McKinstry describing the pain the fire hoses inflicted on the children who marched in the children's crusade*

more than 2,000 protesters, many of them juveniles, were arrested and held in a temporary camp at the Alabama State fairgrounds.[7]

Millions of Americans witnessed the shocking images of violence on television from the Birmingham campaign. They saw graphic photos in newspapers and magazines of children being beaten and attacked by police dogs. Many people who had previously remained unmoved by the civil rights struggle were horrified by the brutality against defenseless children. As Shuttlesworth and others had originally hoped, Birmingham's racist leaders had met nonviolent protest with intense violence—and the whole world was watching.

Not everyone applauded King's nonviolent approach, however—even fellow civil rights leaders. One very public opponent to King's approach was a leader of the Black Nationalist movement, Malcolm X. He proposed that black people fight racial bigotry with self-defense, including armed resistance if necessary. His defiant message gained him followers as the decade progressed.

For the time being, King's approach of nonviolent demonstration in Birmingham brought some success. By May 10, Birmingham city leaders and businessmen worked out an agreement for Birmingham to integrate its downtown and even hire black workers for city jobs. It appeared the Birmingham protest was over.

But Connor was furious that the protesters had won. And so was the KKK, which immediately made a violent scene in Birmingham. On the eve of the agreement, bombs ripped through the home of King's brother, who was involved in the civil rights movement and lived just outside Birmingham. Bombs also

## NONVIOLENT RESISTANCE

King's nonviolent approach was strongly influenced by the example of Mohandas Gandhi, also called Mahatma Gandhi. Gandhi was the leader of the people of India during their struggle for independence from British rule in the early 1900s. King saw that struggle as a mirror of the one he and black Americans were fighting. He also believed in Gandhi's main tactic, nonviolent resistance. This was the basis of every boycott, march, sit-in, and demonstration King led. Some black leaders, such as Malcolm X, saw the approach as immoral and ineffective, but King steadfastly held to it as the backbone of his life and work. As he once said, "Violence solves no social problems; it merely creates new and more complicated ones."[9]

hit the hotel where King and others were staying during the protests. No one was seriously hurt, but in retaliation, angry black demonstrators threw rocks and bottles at Birmingham police before order was restored. To ensure peace, President Kennedy sent a small group of federal troops to a military base outside Birmingham.

The events in Birmingham also moved the president to take legislative action. On June 11, President Kennedy went on television and informed the nation he was sending a new civil rights bill to Congress. This law would finally give all Americans the right to enter any public facility and provided the federal government strong tools to enforce the desegregation of schools.

Just hours after the president's speech, Medgar Evers, the NAACP's field secretary in Mississippi, was murdered at his home. Evers's death dimmed the bright, hopeful spirit the president's speech had created in the black community. It made many people wonder if even the strongest civil rights law in history could really put an end to racial violence in the United States. ●

**Mourners marched in nonviolent solidarity after »
the funeral of civil rights leader Medgar Evers.**

## CHAPTER 5

# FREE AT LAST?

hen President Kennedy's civil rights bill went to Congress in June 1963, various black organizations decided to mark the occasion with a dramatic march on Washington, DC. It would be a massive, nonviolent way to demonstrate unity and show legislators how urgent they considered passage of the law to be.

On August 28, 1963, more than 250,000 white and black people swarmed the nation's capital.[1] It was the largest single demonstration in human rights history in the United States up to this time. Musicians popular at the time gave performances, including singer Joan Baez, who led the crowd in singing "We Shall Overcome" and other protest songs.

Leaders of several black organizations, including the SNCC, CORE, and the NAACP, made stirring and inspiring speeches. The tone of the demonstration and of the crowd was mainly harmonious and hopeful. King was present, and his words captured the sentiment profoundly. That day, at the foot of the Lincoln Memorial, King delivered to the massive crowd a speech that had many biblical and historical references.

## "WE SHALL OVERCOME"

Black Americans have a long history of expressing their troubles through song. Slaves sang to dampen sorrows, lighten work, and celebrate victories. Songs also became an important part of the black civil rights movement, especially "We Shall Overcome." The exact origins of the song are unclear, but American folk singer Pete Seeger is credited with writing the familiar words to the song. It begins:

*We shall overcome,*
*we shall overcome,*

*We shall*
*overcome someday;*

*Oh, deep in my heart,*
*I do believe,*

*We shall overcome*
*someday.*[2]

**VOICES OF THE MOVEMENT**

An excerpt from King's "I Have a Dream" speech in Washington, DC, on August 28, 1963:

**" I have a dream that one day every valley shall be exalted, every hill and mountain shall be made low, the rough places will be made plain, and the crooked places will be made straight, and the glory of the Lord shall be revealed. . . .**

**This is our hope. This is the faith that I go back to the South with. . . . With this faith we will be able to work together, to pray together, to struggle together, to go to jail together, to stand up for freedom together, knowing that we will be free one day. . . .**

**And when this happens, when we allow freedom to ring, when we let it ring from every village and every hamlet, from every state and every city, we will be able to speed up that day when all of God's children . . . will be able to join hands and sing in the words of the old Negro spiritual, "Free at last! free at last! thank God Almighty, we are free at last! "** [3]

It was a soaring tribute to the past and a ringing call for unity and freedom in the future. King's speech that day included the words "I have a dream," which became its eternal title.[4] His speech was the one most people present that day remembered afterward—and it is still remembered and quoted today.

The March on Washington was a resounding success. Because it was carefully controlled by its organizers, there were few incidents of attacks or mistreatment reported by the hundreds of thousands attendees. Some black leaders, most notably Malcolm X, found the interracial tone of the event unfortunate, however. They felt whites had not shared equally in the suffering blacks had during slavery and the civil rights battle and thought it unfair they should share in the glory now. But for most people, the interracial gathering of the march presented an idyllic picture of what the United States could be if people came together in a spirit of

"Who ever heard of angry revolutionists all harmonizing 'We Shall Overcome . . .' while tripping and swaying along arm-in-arm with the very people they were supposed to be angrily revolting against? Who ever heard of angry revolutionists swinging their bare feet together with their oppressor in lily-pad park pools, with gospels and guitars and 'I Have A Dream' speeches?"[5]

—Malcolm X in 1964, speaking about the March on Washington

unity and love. However, those ideals and hopes came crashing down soon after.

## THE CIVIL RIGHTS BILL OF 1964

On September 15, just three weeks after the March on Washington, white supremacists exploded a powerful bomb at Birmingham's Sixteenth Street Baptist Church. Four black children were killed in the blast. That same evening, two black men were murdered in Birmingham streets. The pleasant picture of people of all races singing and celebrating happily together at the march faded in many minds.

Legislators in Washington, DC, debated the civil rights bill all summer and into the fall. Southern senators were blocking it, and many observers began to doubt the bill would ever pass.

Then, on November 22, 1963, President Kennedy was assassinated in Dallas, Texas. Vice President Lyndon B. Johnson became the president. In one of his first speeches in the new role, President Johnson expressed his determination to make sure the civil rights bill President Kennedy sent to Congress was passed.

Johnson's behind-the-scenes maneuvering to convince political parties to pass the bill was relentless and masterful. Along with Senator Hubert Humphrey of Minnesota, who later became President Johnson's vice president, the president rallied religious, civic, and business groups in support of the measure. Although Southern senators used tactics to delay action, the president's supporters in Congress, with the backing of the majority of Americans, passed the bill.

> "We have talked long enough in this country about equal rights. We have talked for one hundred years or more. It is time now to write the next chapter, and to write it in the books of law."[8]
>
> —President Lyndon B. Johnson in a speech before Congress, November 27, 1963

President Johnson signed the new bill into law on July 2, 1964. The nationally televised ceremony was held in the East Room of the White House, where more than 100 guests watched him sign the bill.[6] In keeping with tradition, the president paused after each stroke, turned, and handed the pen he used to special guests standing behind him. It is estimated he went through more than 75 pens signing the bill.[7] One of the first pens he gave away went to King, who received it with obvious delight.

The strongest civil rights law in US history intensified penalties against states and businesses that denied civil rights to persons based on race. One of the most important ways it did this was to give the government the ability to withhold federal money from states that refused to

**King receives an honorary pen President Johnson used to sign the Civil Rights Bill on July 2, 1964.**

obey the law. This meant Southern school systems that had previously blocked black students from enrolling would have to integrate or lose government funding. This financial weapon in itself effectively ended most of the Jim Crow laws still practiced in Southern states. The law also succeeded in opening public accommodations such as restaurants, movie theaters, and sporting events to African Americans.

# FREEDOM SUMMER

One thing the new civil rights law did not adequately address was voting rights. Although the Fifteenth Amendment had been ratified in 1870 giving African Americans the right to vote, Southern authorities had long used a variety of tactics to keep them from voting. The main strategy was simply to keep blacks from registering in the first place. Into the early 1960s, Southern officials used literacy tests in a discriminatory fashion to keep qualified blacks from registering to vote. White registration officials also kept blacks from registering by keeping short office hours and making black people stand in long lines. Then, if all else failed, intimidation and violence were also used to keep black people from signing up to vote. In Mississippi at that time, only approximately 6 percent of the state's black citizens were registered to vote.[9] A coalition of civil rights groups decided to do something about it.

In the summer of 1964, Freedom Summer was organized and led by the SNCC and CORE, with the participation of the SCLC and the NAACP. It was an ambitious campaign to register black voters, provide alternative education for black children and adults, and improve the lives of black Mississippians. The project mobilized approximately 800 white and black Northern volunteers.[10] They would travel to Mississippi and live

A Freedom Summer volunteer teaches a class in Jackson, Mississippi, in the summer of 1964.

in black communities, encouraging people to register and vote. The volunteers were trained to help black men and women read and fill out the intentionally confusing registration forms. The volunteers would then follow their charges to the clerks' offices to be sure the completed forms were accepted and processed.

Freedom Summer included programs called freedom schools, as well, to tutor black children in reading and math. Volunteers also set up centers in black communities where adults could go to get medical and legal assistance. Civil rights leaders were excited about the possibilities of making Mississippi a model for programs all over the nation.

But the program got off to a deadly start. Two hundred eager Freedom Summer workers left Ohio for

Mississippi on June 20.[11] The very next day, three of them were reported missing—two white men, Michael Schwerner and Andrew Goodman, and one black man, James Cheney. When a search failed to locate them after several days, a group of volunteers left the program. But the majority stayed.

Violence and threats also surrounded the program. Cars carrying Freedom Summer workers were shot at. A black church where classes were held was burned. Volunteers were arrested for distributing voter information. Mississippi passed a law making it illegal for the volunteers to teach at freedom schools.

In early August, the bodies of the three missing men were found, brutally murdered. The president instructed the FBI to find the killers. After a successful manhunt, the state of Mississippi refused to prosecute the accused murderers. But the federal government did prosecute and convict a deputy sheriff and several KKK members for civil rights violations. One murderer was convicted in 2005.

None of these things stopped the Freedom Summer volunteers. Many of the projects started during that summer continued in Mississippi and spread nationally. Today's successful preschool educational program Head Start, for example, began as a direct extension of freedom schools. Freedom Summer brought medical, educational, and cultural activities to many black children and adults for the first time in their lives. It brought hope where none had existed before.

Freedom Summer also created the interracial Mississippi Freedom Democratic Party (MFDP). The MFDP challenged the legitimacy of the all-white Mississippi Democratic Party that represented the state at the 1964 Democratic presidential nominating convention. MFDP leader Fannie Lou Hamer spoke before the convention about the depth of racism in Mississippi and the white Democratic Party. Although her televised testimony was riveting, President Johnson worked out a compromise that failed to give the MFDP all that it wanted. Nevertheless, the convention agreed that in the future, no state delegation would be allowed to attend the convention if it discriminated against African Americans or any other minority group. Four years later, in 1968, an interracial delegation from Mississippi, including members of the MFDP, was seated. ●

Members of the Mississippi Freedom »
Democratic Party demonstrated outside the
Democratic National Convention in 1964.

## CHAPTER 6

# THE KEY TO THE DOOR OF FREEDOM

Freedom Summer in Mississippi showed the time was right to push for voting rights in other places, such as Selma, in Alabama's Dallas County. Black residents there had systematically been denied the opportunity to register to vote for years through police intimidation, threats of violence, and confusing registration forms. The SNCC and locals in Selma had

been organizing protests for years without much success,
in part because the federal government refused to provide
protection. The Justice Department also filed voting rights
suits, which moved slowly and were often rejected by
Southern federal judges.

In early January 1965, King and the SCLC arrived
in Selma to lead residents in a protest march. King had
recently been awarded the Nobel Peace Prize for his
civil rights work and was now an international celebrity.
News teams from all over the world followed him to
Selma to document the
demonstration. At a
news conference, King
made it clear the purpose
of the demonstration
was to call attention
nonviolently to the
county's continued
denial of black citizens'
voting rights. To do
this, he and the locals
who joined him would
stage peaceful marches
to county courthouses.
He expressed hope that

"I accept the Nobel Prize
for Peace at a moment when
22 million Negroes of the United
States of America are engaged
in a creative battle to end the
long night of racial injustice. I
accept this award on behalf of a
civil rights movement which is
moving with determination and
a majestic scorn for risk and
danger to establish a reign of
freedom and a rule of justice."[1]

—Martin Luther King Jr. accepting
his Nobel Peace Prize in Oslo,
Norway, December 10, 1964

officials would cooperate and allow thousands of black citizens to register. But his main hope was that the protest would encourage Washington to outlaw discriminatory voter registration requirements once and for all.

## BLOODY SUNDAY

On January 18, King and a group of demonstrators marched to the county courthouse in downtown Selma. They were blocked and arrested by police. Protesters by the thousands poured into Selma's streets in the coming weeks. By early February, more than 2,400 protesters had been arrested.[2] From jail, King sent a letter to the *New York Times* stating there were more people in Dallas County's cells than there were black people registered to vote in Selma. In a subsequent demonstration in a neighboring town, a peaceful black protester, Jimmie Lee Jackson, was shot and killed by state police. His death incited the local black community. It convinced King to plan a more dramatic protest.

When they were released from jail in early February, King and the Selma demonstrators announced a plan to march 50 miles (80 km) from Selma to the state capital of Montgomery to demand equal voting rights. Although King helped plan the march, he did not lead it. On March 7, with King away in Atlanta, approximately 600 black marchers left Selma and headed east on US

**Police struck protesters with clubs on Bloody Sunday.**

Highway 80 toward Montgomery.[3] The protesters met
no resistance—until they crossed the Edmund Pettus
Bridge over the Alabama River. On the other side stood a
huge number of Alabama state troopers and the forces of
the Dallas County sheriff. When marchers did not stop,
troopers moved forward and began shoving and beating
them with clubs. Some troopers fired tear gas while others
on horseback charged into the crowd. People were knocked
down, trampled, and bloodied. Seventeen marchers were
taken to the hospital.[4]

Television stations all over the country interrupted
regular programming to show film footage of "Bloody
Sunday," as the event came to be known. A federal judge
issued an order forbidding the Selma demonstrators to
complete the march. But King, now back in Selma, and his
fellow marchers refused to listen.

## A BRIDGE TO FREEDOM

Two days later, King led more than 2,000 black and white marchers out of Selma onto the Edmund Pettus Bridge.[5] There, he paused, bowed, and prayed. Watching from the other side were hundreds of state troopers armed with clubs and tear gas. Then, to the surprise of thousands, King rose, turned, and began leading the massive march back into Selma. He later said he could not in good conscience violate a federal court order or lead his people into another bloody encounter. However, one of the marchers, Reverend James Reeb, was beaten and killed on a Selma street by a group of white attackers.

On March 15, with tensions in Selma escalating, President Johnson presented before Congress his proposal for a new voting rights act. The speech he delivered was a resounding call to the nation to support the ongoing struggle of its black citizens to secure the right to vote. When Johnson ended with the words "We shall overcome," it was an emotional moment for the protesters watching on television back in Selma.[6] Johnson's "We Shall Overcome" speech is considered a landmark in the history of civil rights.

The next week, King received word the federal judge had lifted the ban on the march. President Johnson activated approximately 3,000 federal troops and marshals

An excerpt from
President Lyndon B.
Johnson's speech to
Congress on March 15,
1965, concerning his
intention to present a
voting rights bill:

VOICES
OF THE
MOVEMENT

"We cannot, we
must not, refuse to protect the right of every
American to vote in every election that he may
desire to participate in.

And we ought not, and we cannot, and we must
not wait another eight months before we get
a bill. We have already waited 100 years and
more and the time for waiting is gone. . . .

But even if we pass this bill the battle will not
be over. What happened in Selma is part of a
far larger movement which reaches into every
section and state of America. It is the effort of
American Negroes to secure for themselves the
full blessings of American life. Their cause must
be our cause too. Because it's not just Negroes,
but really it's all of us, who must overcome the
crippling legacy of bigotry and injustice. And we
shall overcome."[7]

in Alabama and ordered them to escort the marchers to Montgomery.[8]

So, on March 21, when approximately 4,000 black and white marchers set out, for a third time, to cross the Edmund Pettus Bridge, soldiers lined the highway to protect them.[9] The massive group spent nights in tents and on the roadside. Volunteers and people who lived along the way gave them food and water. Thousands from all over the country joined the march, and everyone seemed buoyed by a spirit of unity and cooperation. By the time the first marchers entered Montgomery five days later, 25,000 black and white people were walking together.[10]

The hope and joy of the occasion did not last to the next day, however. It was dampened that night when a white woman from Detroit, Michigan, Viola Liuzzo, was shot and killed while driving black marchers from Montgomery back to Selma. KKK members spotted her with a black man in her car and became enraged, chasing the car and shooting. The KKK members responsible for the crime were quickly arrested. But local juries could not reach an agreement, and the KKK members were not charged with murder at the trial. The men were convicted on federal charges of civil rights violations, however. Liuzzo's murder also led the president to reinvestigate the

**Thousands of civil rights marchers triumphantly crossed »
the Edmund Pettus Bridge on March 21, 1965.**

Heading to the trial, the white defense attorney representing Viola Liuzzo's murderers awkwardly rode the elevator with Liuzzo's passenger from the night of her murder.

KKK. But while it saddened the civil rights community, the murder did not stop the movement—or the voting rights bill.

In August, President Johnson signed that bill into law. The law abolished unfair policies and practices that had kept eligible black Americans from registering to vote or actually voting. It was, as President Johnson put it, "one of the most monumental laws in the entire history of American freedom."[11] ●

## VOTING RIGHTS ACT OF 1965

The Voting Rights Act of 1965 provided the federal government with potent tools to extend voting rights to eligible blacks. It suspended literacy tests and dispatched federal officials to help blacks register in the South. The law also prohibited states that had discriminated against black people from changing their voting laws in the future without first getting permission from the federal government. With the 1965 law in place, the percentage of black people on voter registration lists in many Southern states skyrocketed. In just months, the number of registered black voters in Alabama, Mississippi, and Louisiana increased by a total of 430,000. In Mississippi alone, the number jumped from 22,000 to 150,000 in only three months.[12] Black voter registration continued to increase in following years. Mississippi black voter registration shot from 6 percent in 1964 to 60 percent four years later, and Alabama rose from 23 percent to 57 percent during this same period.[13]

## CHAPTER 7
— — —

# DAYS OF RAGE: BURN, BABY, BURN!

T hough steps toward equality had been established, the fight for civil rights raged on through the mid-to-late 1960s. Years of oppression and torment boiled over in the form of fights, arrests, and riots between black and white communities.

In the summer of 1965, people in the mostly black community of Watts, California, sweltered in the heat. They were smoldering inside as well. All it took was one small spark to ignite the whole south-central Los Angeles neighborhood.

The afternoon of August 11, five days after passage of the monumental Voting Rights Act, a black man driving under the influence of alcohol was pulled over and arrested by police. Members of his family were at the scene, and a crowd gathered to watch as they confronted the police. The interaction became hostile. Shouting erupted into an ugly street battle between white cops and black residents. Police responded to physical threats and punches with an exaggerated show of force. Shots were fired. Within minutes, enraged black men and women swarmed the block and began fighting with the police. Black members of the community beat many whites who entered the area. By nightfall, the entire commercial center of Watts had exploded into a full-blown riot that continued unchecked for six days. By the time it was over, rioters had burned automobiles, looted stores, and damaged or destroyed millions of dollars in property and goods. Thirty-four people died, more than 1,000 were injured, and close to 4,000 were arrested.[1]

Public officials claimed the riot was caused by outside agitators. But it was later recognized the real cause was widespread desperation and feelings of helplessness in the face of racism and economic injustice. Many black people in the urban ghettos of the North and West had not been oppressed by Jim Crow laws or the KKK. Many in these areas also had long had the right to vote and had elected some black officials to city councils, state legislatures, and Congress. But their lives had not improved materially, and changes that occurred did not meet their expectations. They still encountered police brutality, segregation, inferior schools, and employment discrimination. This gnawed away at black people's sense of justice and self-worth for years. By the mid-1960s, there was little room left for anything but rage. Watts was only the beginning.

## BLACK POWER

The sense of anger and desperation that fueled these outbreaks transformed the civil rights movement. The beliefs Malcolm X had voiced earlier in the decade earned him many followers as the 1960s continued, and he became one of the most recognized leaders of the new, more aggressive civil rights movement. Representatives of this group included Stokely Carmichael and H. Rap Brown of the SNCC; Floyd McKissick, president of CORE;

An excerpt from
a speech given by
Malcolm X on
February 14, 1965:

**VOICES
OF THE
MOVEMENT**

"When somebody stands up and talks like I just did, they say, 'Why, he's advocating violence!' . . . I have never advocated any violence. I've only said that Black people who are the victims of organized violence . . . should defend ourselves. And when I say that we should defend ourselves against the violence of others, they use their press skillfully to make the world think that I'm calling on violence, period. I wouldn't call on anybody to be violent without a cause. But I think the Black man in this country, above and beyond people all over the world, will be more justified when he stands up and starts to protect himself. . . .

I don't believe in violence—that's why I want to stop it. And you can't stop it with love . . . . So, we only mean vigorous action in self-defense, and that vigorous action we feel we're justified in initiating by any means necessary."[2]

## MALCOLM X

Malcolm X was born Malcolm Little in 1925. As a young adult, he converted to Islam. Following his conversion, he dropped his last name and replaced it with X, becoming Malcolm X. Malcolm X attracted a large following with his call for Black Nationalism. Malcolm X's words and work represent the roots of the Black Power movement that gained momentum in the 1960s. He preached self-defense and self-determination for African Americans and denounced white people and institutions as evil. Malcolm X was a minister in the Nation of Islam, a radical black organization outside of the traditional Muslim faith. By the end of his life, however, he broke away from the Nation of Islam and embraced the traditional Muslim religion. He also refrained from denouncing all whites, and he sought alliances with King and other civil rights leaders without abandoning his core belief in black self-determination. Malcolm X was murdered in 1965 by black opponents from the Nation of Islam while speaking in Harlem, but his ideas live on today.

and Eldridge Cleaver, author of *Soul On Ice*, a book that raged against white racism.

Many of Malcolm X's followers remained loyal to his message even after his assassination in 1965. In 1966, Carmichael and McKissick energized the SNCC's new young members with an updated, more aggressive version of Malcolm X's message of black pride and self-defense. This stemmed from an unraveling of the civil rights coalition between these more radical groups and nonviolent groups led by King. During a march co-led by King, Carmichael and McKissick discovered

**Malcolm X's powerful speeches and calls to action jolted the civil rights movement in a new direction.**

they could fire up young crowds with the chant, "Black Power! Black Power!"[3] Newspapers printed the catchphrase as a headline the next day. *Black Power* quickly became the term used to describe the new, militant direction of the more radical civil rights movement.

Leaders of the new movement challenged the nonviolent tactics of King, viewing them as weak and ineffective. They disagreed with King that black people should focus on integration or unite with or rely on white leaders and legislators. They also believed blacks had suffered and waited too long for whites to hand them their rights. It was time for blacks to control their own destiny.

## BLACK POWER: THE BLACK PANTHERS

In 1966, at the height of the Black Power movement, California college students Huey Newton and Bobby Seale founded the Black Panther Party for Self-Defense. It was created as a way for poor black people to fight back against police mistreatment. Black Panthers took to the streets carrying guns and wearing black leather jackets and berets. They saw themselves as revolutionaries, confronting a corrupt, unjust white system. The media emphasized the Panthers' military characteristics while ignoring the group's positive efforts, such as setting up free breakfast programs and free medical care in many urban black communities. Law enforcement agencies in cooperation with the FBI made it nearly impossible for the Black Panthers to accomplish their goals, harassing, infiltrating, and spying on the group.

Carmichael asserted that the civil rights movement until then had tried to make blacks more like whites. He urged young African Americans to embrace their African roots and love themselves for what they were. Carmichael and his followers believed that in order to amass sufficient power, black people had to control their own communities politically and economically. Only then, they believed, would blacks be able to negotiate with whites on an equal basis. The SNCC was one of the first groups to ask

A white protester assaulted a black man who had been shot in the stomach during the Detroit riots as the man was escorted from the scene by police officers.

its white members to leave so it could become an all-black organization.

Rioting continued during this time. In 1967, fiery riots rocked more than 100 cities across the United States. The worst of these were in Newark, New Jersey, and Detroit. In Detroit alone, the civil strife lasted one week and resulted in 43 deaths—33 black and 10 white—and more than 2,000 injured.[4] The title of a popular song at the time, "Burn, Baby, Burn," became a popular refrain throughout the ghettos.[5] The riots were spontaneous uprisings, but for many they were an act of rebellion. The National Commission on Civil Disorders, known as the Kerner Commission and established by President Johnson, issued a report on the riots. It blamed white racism and the conditions it produced for the riots.

# "I'VE SEEN THE PROMISED LAND"

By 1968, it was clear the classic civil rights movement had split into two opposing camps. With the Civil Rights Act of 1964 and the Voting Rights Act of 1965, many of the goals of the original movement had been met. But urban violence and continued racism and poverty affecting black people throughout the nation proved the struggle for equality was far from over. In an effort to keep his nonviolent campaign moving forward, King began expanding his vision to meet the remaining challenges of racial equality. He and his SCLC followers attacked social evils such as hunger, poverty, and substandard living conditions. He also spoke against the Vietnam War (1955–1975).

In March 1968, King received a plea to go to Memphis, Tennessee, to lead a protest by black sanitation workers on strike over poor wages and treatment. King agreed. When he arrived in Memphis for the protest, gangs of young black men began rioting in the city. This upset King. White authorities reacted with a show of force. They brought in thousands of National Guard troops, who tamped down the looting and fires with tear gas and guns. King and the union strikers he came to lead were blamed for the furor, even though they took no part in the riot. King was determined to regain control and

**King spoke at the Mason Temple in Memphis, Tennessee, on April 3, 1968, in his last public appearance.**

illustrate that he still held true to his original philosophy of nonviolent resistance.

On April 3, 1968, King stood before a group at a Memphis church to speak about his plans for continuing the protest. He urged his audience to act in a responsible, nonviolent way. He spoke of the long road he had traveled on his quest for equality and justice for his people. He ended with words that would later seem eerily prophetic:

*We've got some difficult days ahead. But it really doesn't matter to me now. . . . I just want to do*

*God's will. And he's allowed me to go up on the*
*mountain. And I've looked over and I've seen the*
*Promised Land. So, I'm happy tonight. I'm not*
*worried about anything. I'm not fearing any man.*[6]

The next day, as King stood on a balcony outside his hotel room talking to friends, he was struck in the head by a bullet. An hour later, he died at a Memphis hospital. King's death sent shock waves through the nation. Rioting erupted in many cities. And although a white man named James Earl Ray was convicted, questions remained as to whether there was a conspiracy behind King's murder.

The day after King's death, President Johnson sent a letter to congressional leaders. He urged them to pass the Civil Rights Bill of 1968, which was working its way through the national legislature, in King's memory. The law would make it illegal to deny housing to people based on their race, religion, or national origin. Known as the Fair Housing Act, the law had been stalled in Congress for some time. Upon President

**"If you give your life to a cause in which you believe, and if it is right and just, and if your life comes to an end as a result of this, then your life could not have been spent in a more redemptive way. I think that is what my husband has done."**[7]

—*Coretta Scott King, leading a march in Memphis, Tennessee, on April 9, 1968, five days after her husband's death*

Johnson's urging, it was enacted on April 11, just one week after King's death.

The impact King's assassination had on the American civil rights moment was immense. After his passing, no other leaders of the nonviolent movement were able to inspire or unite people as King had. Nevertheless, in towns and villages throughout the South, black people continued to struggle for their civil rights.

Although many issues remained unsolved, a number of the original goals King and his colleagues set had been reached. As the 1970s dawned, the general impression in the United States was that King's death signaled an end of the classic black civil rights movement. Society was changing, and while black civil rights were still on many people's minds, so were other issues, such as the Vietnam War and women's rights. ●

## MARTIN LUTHER KING JR. DAY

Shortly after King's death, a bill was introduced in Congress proposing a special day be set aside in his memory. Fifteen years later, on November 3, 1983, President Ronald Reagan signed the bill into law. The third Monday in January each year became a federal holiday, Martin Luther King Jr. Day. The day was first officially observed on January 20, 1986.

CHAPTER 8

# CIVIL RIGHTS BEYOND THE 1960s

In the 1970s, despite the progress made in the two previous decades, the quality of life for many black Americans still lagged behind that of white Americans. The Civil Rights Act of 1964 banned discrimination by employers against any person because of race, color, or sex. The law also stated that public schools and universities must enroll any qualified student who applied. But the reality in the decades following was that black people still faced discrimination in employment and housing. And the percentage of black students attending colleges and universities was far lower than their percentage in the general population. Many public elementary and high schools remained racially unbalanced as well, and fewer black students were graduating than whites. Blacks also occupied a smaller percentage of elected political offices than their proportion of the adult population. It became obvious that simply saying people are equal did not immediately make it so.

The reasons behind the inequality at the time were complex but boiled down to one thing: a systematic lack of opportunity. Black Americans simply had more obstacles to overcome than white Americans did, and the effects of past discrimination were embedded in the fabric of society. Black Americans did not gain their full legal rights as citizens until 1965. As President Johnson said that year,

> You do not take a person who for years has been hobbled by chains and liberate him, bring him up to the starting line of a race and then say, 'You are free to compete with all the others,' and still justly believe you have been completely fair."[1]

## BLACK REPARATIONS

Some black organizations made claims during the civil rights movement that white people and institutions should pay African Americans monetary reparations for their mistreatment during slavery and after. SNCC leader James Forman issued his "Black Manifesto" in 1969. In it he called for white churches to collect $500 million in reparations.[2] In 1993, law professor Boris Bittker took up the matter. Since then, bills have been introduced in Congress calling for black reparations, but none have passed.

Fairness meant finding ways to allow everyone to compete equally to overcome the effects of discrimination. One solution was affirmative action. This was a term used by President Johnson to describe a set of programs designed to increase opportunities for qualified blacks in employment and admission to higher education. Affirmative action included policies that set goals for hiring minorities, and subsequently women, for jobs and admission to colleges and universities. The programs continued under President Richard Nixon in the early 1970s and became a model for policies most US businesses adopted in the 1970s and 1980s. In 1978, the Supreme Court upheld affirmative action in the case of *University of California Regents v. Bakke* but rejected the use of fixed numbers of employees or students based on race.

Not everyone then or now agrees about the effectiveness or fairness of affirmative action. Many people, mostly white men and a smaller proportion of women and black people, saw its policies as "reverse discrimination," as white males in particular were passed over for jobs in favor of hiring black people or women who were allegedly less qualified. The legal issues of affirmative action are complex. Some states, such as California, have passed laws against it. Some people believe the impact of affirmative action programs has been small at best. Others state that, despite its faults, affirmative action remains the most effective way to make up for years of discrimination against minorities.

Whether due to affirmative action or abolishing segregation, employment has improved for the black population. In 1940, 5.2 percent of black men and 6.4 percent of black women worked in well-paying white-collar jobs, for example as managers, clerks, teachers, and accountants. By the mid-1990s, 32 percent of black men and approximately 59 percent of black women held those jobs.[3] Average incomes rose as a result. In 1960, a black family with two parents earned 61 percent as much as the average two-parent white family.[4] In 1995, that number rose to 87 percent.[5] Things continued to improve at a rapid rate. In 1997, the unemployment rate among African Americans dropped below 10 percent, which was the lowest in 27 years.[6] One black congresswoman attributed the improvement to affirmative action: "Affirmative action, by all statistical measures, has been the central ingredient to the creation of the Black middle class."[7]

Affirmative action also affected the integration of schools. In 1964, ten years after *Brown v. Board of Education of Topeka,* a government investigation revealed that only 2.4 percent of black children in the South were attending white schools, and that segregated schools were still the norm in other parts of the nation as well.[8] The Civil Rights Act of 1964 ordered that new guidelines be established to ensure the rate of school desegregation would increase. In 1966, the Department of Health, Education, and Welfare (HEW) determined that 16 to 18 percent of African-American children in all public school districts must attend predominantly white schools.[9] In 1968, the Supreme Court ruled that school districts could begin busing a certain number of black and white students from their neighborhood schools to other areas to meet the HEW requirements.

Using busing to achieve racial desegregation in schools was controversial from the start and quickly created a whole new set of political and social issues. By 2010, the courts had largely struck down busing. Many schools still remain somewhat segregated today due to

Many opponents of affirmative action feel it is reverse racism against the white population. Marchers protested forced busing of black students to white schools in Boston in 1975.

residential segregation and the creation of private schools to avoid desegregation.

Disturbing patterns of poverty and discrimination also still affect millions of black Americans. A new form of racism emerged in the 2000s, which one writer referred to as "the prison industrial complex," or "bodies destined for profitable punishment."[10] These terms describe the

## CIVIL RIGHTS IN THE 1970s AND 1980s: JESSE JACKSON

The Reverend Jesse Jackson was one of King's most trusted aides. In the 1970s and 1980s, Jackson achieved national status as a civil rights leader in his own right. His charismatic personality and positive message for young black children, particularly the urban poor, inspired many people of all races. Jackson created a "Rainbow Coalition" which successfully continued King's legacy of interracial cooperation and unity in politics. Jackson ran for president twice as the first major black candidate, but fell short both times. His stirring address at the 1988 Democratic National Convention ended with the words "Keep hope alive."[13] Those words became the slogan for Jackson's candidacy and his ongoing work afterward. Jackson continues to play an important role in black affairs and national politics today.

United States' massive penal, or prison, system, in which large numbers of young black people are routinely placed in prisons that operate as efficient factories. Built and operated by large corporations, these prisons produce millions of dollars in goods and materials each year, all generated by the toil of a steady supply of free labor: the prisoners. Of the more than 2 million prisoners, nearly two-thirds are young, uneducated black men and women.[11] The higher ratio of black people being arrested and trapped in the penal system is a situation one author called "the new Jim Crow."[12]

# "THE AUDACITY OF HOPE"

While the struggle for total equality continues for many black Americans, there have been major strides forward. The Reverend Jesse Jackson became an iconic leader of the movement in the 1970s and 1980s, especially when he ran for the Democratic Party's presidential nomination. Although he lost, Jackson did inspire hope and more black voter registration. During the 1980s and 1990s, the election of black mayors, police chiefs, and councilmen and councilwomen, and the appointment of black Americans to important national governmental position signaled a shift in attitude throughout the nation.

On November 4, 2008, the nation's first black president was elected. Illinois senator Barack Obama burst onto the national scene in July 2004 with an electrifying speech at the Democratic National Convention. In his speech, he implied that the boldness of those whose fight for civil rights had made it possible for him to be where he was. Obama called the spirit of these people "the audacity of hope."[14] Obama's election fulfilled a dream many had hoped would come true. As one writer said, President Obama was "not the seed but the flower of the civil rights movement."[15]

Despite this milestone, the struggle for black civil rights continues today. Many black leaders continue to insist the United States live up to the promises of complete

## EMOTIONAL ELECTION

At the time of President Obama's election, the only living speaker from the March on Washington in 1963 was Democratic congressman John Lewis. As a former chairman of the SNCC, Lewis had taken part in Freedom Rides, sit-ins, and voter registration drives in the 1960s. Witnessing President Obama's election was an emotional moment for many people who lived through the civil rights movement, including Lewis. He said, "If someone had told me this would be happening now, I would have told them they were crazy. . . . To the people who were beaten, put in jail, were asked questions they could never answer to register to vote, it's amazing."[16]

civil rights and equality made to all citizens in the Declaration of Independence and the Constitution. Until those promises are met for everyone, in every aspect of life, the journey to total freedom continues. ●

**President Barack Obama, *left*, and Reverend »
Jesse Jackson, *right*, emerged as modern
leaders of today's civil rights movement.**

**LATE 1800s** Jim Crow laws in the South segregate black and white people.

**1896** The Supreme Court rules in *Plessy v. Ferguson* that "separate but equal" railroad car facilities are constitutional.

**1947** The President's Committee on Civil Rights recommends an end to segregation and expansion of the right to vote.

**1954** On May 17, the US Supreme Court rules in *Brown v. Board of Education of Topeka* that "separate but equal" is invalid in US schools.

**1955** Fourteen-year-old Emmett Till is murdered in Mississippi on August 28. His death and the acquittal of his killers influence the next generation of civil rights activists.

**1955** Rosa Parks is arrested for refusing to give up her bus seat on December 1, sparking the Montgomery, Alabama, bus boycott.

**1957** The Civil Rights Act of 1957 is passed.

**1957** The Little Rock Nine attempt and finally integrate an all-white school September 4–25, amid violent riots aiming to prevent their doing so.

**1960**
Lunch counter sit-ins begin in Greensboro, North Carolina, on February 1 and spread throughout the South.

**1961**
Black and white Freedom Riders integrate buses in Southern states throughout the summer.

**1963**
Martin Luther King Jr. delivers his "I Have a Dream" speech at the Lincoln Memorial during the March on Washington on August 28.

**1964**
President Lyndon B. Johnson signs the Civil Rights Act of 1964 into law on July 2.

**1965**
Protests for voting rights take place in Selma, Alabama, between January and March.

**1965**
The Voting Rights Act of 1965 becomes law on August 6.

**1968**
On April 11, President Johnson signs the Civil Rights Act of 1968.

**1978**
The US Supreme Court upholds affirmative action but rejects racial quotas.

**2008**
Barack Obama is elected the first black US president on November 4.

## PERCENTAGE OF THE BLACK POPULATION IN POVERTY: 2007–2011

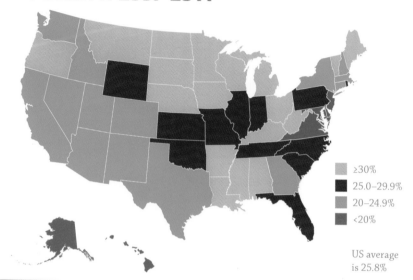

≥30%

25.0–29.9%

20–24.9%

<20%

US average is 25.8%

## DATE OF THE MOVEMENT'S BEGINNING

1950s

## LOCATIONS

The South; Birmingham, Alabama; Chicago, Illinois; Washington, DC; Watts, California; Selma, Alabama; Little Rock, Arkansas

## KEY PLAYERS

**Martin Luther King Jr.** was the most famed leader of the nonviolent black civil rights movement. His impassioned speeches and peaceful demonstrations gave life to the entire movement.

## BLACK ELECTED OFFICIALS IN THE UNITED STATES: 1970–2000

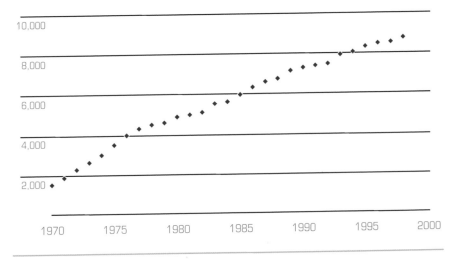

Leader of the Black Nationalist movement, **Malcolm X** opposed a passive nonviolent approach to ending black discrimination, believing instead in demanding equality and obtaining it by any means necessary.

**Lyndon B. Johnson** became president in 1963. He supported the black civil rights movement and was determined to implement laws securing equal rights for all citizens.

## GOALS AND OUTCOMES

The black civil rights movement worked to achieve equality in several areas for black Americans. The fight for complete equality continues today, but the movement in the 1960s brought about sweeping change: segregation was ended, complete voting rights were granted, and discrimination was lessened.

# GLOSSARY

**activist**
  Someone who protests or speaks out against a social, political, economic, or moral wrong.

**affirmative action**
  A program or policy that attempts to correct past discrimination by actively recruiting qualified minorities and women in education and employment.

**agitator**
  Someone who tries to stir up the public.

**Black Nationalism**
  An idea that encourages black people to embrace their heritage and control their own destinies while calling for separatism from whites.

**boycott**
  An organized protest in which someone stops buying or using a certain product or service in order to force the makers or sellers to change the service or product.

**civil rights**
  Rights guaranteed by law to all citizens.

**discrimination**
  Treating a person differently because of the group to which he or she belongs.

**integration**
  The bringing together of different groups into a blended group.

## Jim Crow laws

A set of laws, customs, and regulations in the South that separated blacks from whites to ensure blacks were kept down.

## lynching

The torture and murder of someone without due process of law.

## militant

A tendency to use activist rather than passive means to achieve goals.

## Negro

A term once used to refer to African Americans.

## racist

A person who discriminates or is prejudiced against a person or group due to race or skin color.

## segregation

The separation of one racial group from another or from society.

## sharecropping

Working land owned by someone else in return for food, shelter, and a portion of the crops.

## sit-in

A nonviolent form of protest in which activists occupy seats or spaces normally forbidden to them.

## white supremacy

The belief that the white race is superior to all others.

# ADDITIONAL RESOURCES

## SELECTED BIBLIOGRAPHY

Lawson, Steven F. *Running for Freedom: Civil Rights and Black Politics in America Since 1941*. 3rd ed. Malden, MA: Wiley-Blackwell, 2009. Print.

Powledge, Fred. *Free at Last? The Civil Rights Movement and the People Who Made It*. Boston: Little, 1991. Print.

Tuck, Stephen G. N. *We Ain't What We Ought to Be: The Black Freedom Struggle from Emancipation to Obama*. Cambridge, MA: Belknap Press of Harvard UP, 2010. Print.

Williams, Juan. *Eyes on the Prize: America's Civil Rights Years, 1954–1965*. New York: Viking, 1987. Print.

## FURTHER READINGS

George, Charles, ed. *Living through the Civil Rights Movement*. Detroit: Greenhaven, 2007. Print.

Supples, Kevin. *Speaking Out: The Civil Rights Movement, 1950–1964*. Washington, DC: National Geographic, 2006. Print.

## WEB SITES

To learn more about the civil rights movement, visit ABDO Publishing Company online at **www.abdopublishing.com**. Web sites about the civil rights movement are featured on our Book Links page. These links are routinely monitored and updated to provide the most current information available.

## PLACES TO VISIT

### The Birmingham Civil Rights Institute

520 Sixteenth Street North
Birmingham, AL 35203
205-328-9696, ext. 203
http://www.bcri.org/index.html
The Birmingham Civil Rights Institute includes a museum
with permanent and traveling exhibits depicting the
struggles of the American civil rights movement.

### The National Civil Rights Museum

450 Mulberry Street
Memphis, TN 38103
901-521-9699
http://www.civilrightsmuseum.org
The National Civil Rights Museum is located at the Lorraine
Motel, the assassination site of Martin Luther King Jr. The
museum features key episodes of the American civil rights
movement.

### National Voting Rights Museum and Institute

6 US Highway 80 East
Selma, AL 36701
334-418-0800
http://www.nvrm.org
The National Voting Rights Museum and Institute is located
in Selma, Alabama, at the foot of the famous Edmund Pettus
Bridge, where Bloody Sunday took place. The museum's
galleries and exhibits honor civil rights leaders and warriors.

# SOURCE NOTES

**CHAPTER 1. THE MONTGOMERY BUS BOYCOTT**

1. Jo Ann Gibson Robinson. *The Montgomery Bus Boycott and the Women Who Started It: The Memoir of Jo Ann Gibson Robinson.* Knoxville, TN: U of Tennessee P, 1987. Print. 8.

2. "Rosa Parks." *National Ethnic Coalition of Organizations.* NECO, 2013. Web. 25 Apr. 2013.

**CHAPTER 2. RECONSTRUCTION AND OPPRESSION**

1. "14th Amendment to the US Constitution." *Library of Congress: Primary Documents in American History.* Library of Congress, 24 Aug. 2012. Web. 23 Apr. 2013.

2. "The Chicago Race Riot of 1919." *History.* A&E Television Networks, 2013. Web. 23 Apr. 2013.

3. Ibid.

4. Michael Kazin, Rebecca Edwards, and Adam Rothman, eds. *The Concise Princeton Encyclopedia of American Political History.* Princeton, NJ: Princeton UP, 2011. *Google Book Search.* Web. 23 Apr. 2013.

5. Stephen G. N. Tuck. *We Ain't What We Ought to Be: The Black Freedom Struggle from Emancipation to Obama.* Cambridge, MA: Belknap Press of Harvard UP, 2010. Print. 233.

**CHAPTER 3. SEGREGATION AND EDUCATION**

1. Peter Irons. *Jim Crow's Children: The Broken Promise of the Brown Decision.* New York: Viking, 2002. *Google Book Search.* Web. 24 Apr. 2013.

2. "Plessy v. Ferguson." *Encyclopædia Britannica.* Encyclopædia Britannica, 2013. Web. 23 Apr. 2013.

3. "With All Deliberate Speed." *Smithsonian National Museum of American History: Separate is Not Equal; Brown v Board of Education.* Smithsonian National Museum of American History, n.d. Web. 23 Apr. 2013.

4. "Supreme Court of the United States: Brown v. Board of Education, 347 U.S. 483 (1954) (USSC+)." *National Center for Public Policy Research.* National Center for Public Policy Research, n.d. Web. 23 Apr. 2013.

5. Juan Williams. *Eyes on the Prize: America's Civil Rights Years, 1954–1965.* New York: Viking, 1987. Print. 42.

6. Sanford Wexler. *The Civil Rights Movement: An Eyewitness History.* New York: Checkmark, 1998. Print. 97.

**CHAPTER 4. NEW TACTICS, SAME RESPONSE**

1. Juan Williams. *Eyes on the Prize: America's Civil Rights Years, 1954–1965.* New York: Viking, 1987. Print. 158–159.

2. Fred Powledge. *Free At Last? The Civil Rights Movement and the People Who Made It.* Boston: Little, 1991. Print. 483.

3. Martin Luther King Jr. "16 April 1963 'Letter from Birmingham Jail.'" *Martin Luther King Jr. and the Global Freedom Struggle*. Martin Luther King Jr. Research and Education Institute, n.d. Web. 23 Apr. 2013.

4. Andrew M. Manis. *A Fire You Can't Put Out: The Civil Rights Life of Birmingham's Reverend Fred Shuttlesworth*. Tuscaloosa: U of Alabama P, 1999. Print. 364–368.

5. Sanford Wexler. *The Civil Rights Movement: An Eyewitness History*. New York: Checkmark, 1998. Print. 164.

6. Ibid.

7. Martin Luther King, Jr. *The Autobiography of Martin Luther King, Jr.* New York: Warner, 1998. Print. 208.

8. Juan Williams. *Eyes My Soul Looks Back in Wonder: Voices of the Civil Rights Experience*. New York: AARP-Sterling, 2004. *Google Book Search*. Web. 23 Apr. 2013.

9. Martin Luther King Jr. "Nonviolence and Racial Justice." *American Experience*. WGBH Educational Foundation, 2009. Web. 23 Apr. 2013.

### CHAPTER 5. FREE AT LAST?

1. Fred Powledge. *Free At Last? The Civil Rights Movement and the People Who Made It*. Boston: Little, 1991. Print. 537.

2. "We Shall Overcome." *A Brief History of Music and Race in Twentieth-Century America*. Kansas State U, n.d. Web. 23 Apr. 2013.

3. Martin Luther King Jr. "Martin Luther King's Speech: 'I Have a Dream'; The Full Text." *ABC News*. ABC News, 28 Aug. 1963. Web. 23 Apr. 2013.

4. Juan Williams. *Eyes on the Prize: America's Civil Rights Years, 1954–1965*. New York: Viking, 1987. Print. 200–201.

5. "'The Farce in Washington': A Critique of the March on Washington by Malcolm X 1964." *WGCU: Freedom, A History of US*. Picture History and Educational Broadcasting Corporation, n.d. Web. 23 Apr. 2013.

6. E. W. Kenworthy. "Johnson Signs Voting Rights Bill, Orders Immediate Enforcement 4 Suits Will Challenge Poll Tax." *New York Times: How Race is Lived in America*. New York Times, 7 Aug. 1965. Web. 23 Apr. 2013.

7. Claire Suddath. "Why Did Obama Use So Many Pens to Sign the Health Care Bill?" *Time: Swampland*. Time, 23 Mar. 2010. Web. 23 Apr. 2013.

8. "Landmark Legislation: The Civil Rights Act of 1964." *United States Senate*. US Senate, n.d. Web. 23 Apr. 2013.

9. "Freedom Summer: Three CORE Members Murdered in Mississippi." *CORE*. Congress of Racial Equality, n.d. Web. 23 Apr. 2013.

10. Juan Williams. *Eyes on the Prize: America's Civil Rights Years, 1954–1965*. New York: Viking, 1987. Print. 230.

11. Sanford Wexler. *The Civil Rights Movement: An Eyewitness History*. New York: Checkmark, 1998. Print. 201.

## CHAPTER 6. THE KEY TO THE DOOR OF FREEDOM

1. "The Nobel Peace Prize 1964: Martin Luther King Jr. Acceptance Speech." *Nobelprize.org*. Nobel Media, 10 Dec. 1964. Web. 23 Apr. 2013.

2. Stephen G. N. Tuck. *We Ain't What We Ought to Be: The Black Freedom Struggle from Emancipation to Obama*. Cambridge, MA: Belknap Press of Harvard UP, 2010. Print. 320.

3. "Selma-to-Montgomery March: National Historic Trail and All-American Road." *Nps.gov*. National Park Service, n.d. Web. 23 Apr. 2013.

4. Stephen G. N. Tuck. *We Ain't What We Ought to Be: The Black Freedom Struggle from Emancipation to Obama*. Cambridge, MA: Belknap Press of Harvard UP, 2010. Print. 321.

5. "Selma to Montgomery March (1965)." *Martin Luther King Jr. and the Global Freedom Struggle*. Martin Luther King Jr. Research and Education Institute, n.d. Web. 23 Apr. 2013.

6. Sanford Wexler. *The Civil Rights Movement: An Eyewitness History*. New York: Checkmark, 1998. Print. 222.

7. "Transcript of the Johnson Address on Voting Rights to Joint Session of Congress." *New York Times: Books*. New York Times, 16 Mar. 1965. Web. 23 Apr. 2013.

8. Ralph David Abernathy. *And the Walls Came Tumbling Down: An Autobiography*. New York: Harper, 1989. Print. 348.

9. Juan Williams. *Eyes on the Prize: America's Civil Rights Years, 1954–1965*. New York: Viking, 1987. Print. 279.

10. Ibid. 282–283.

11 Ibid. 285.

12. Fred Powledge. *Free At Last? The Civil Rights Movement and the People Who Made It*. Boston: Little, 1991. Print. 630.

13. Steven F. Lawson. *Running for Freedom: Civil Rights and Black Politics in America Since 1941*. 3rd ed. Malden, MA: Wiley-Blackwell, 2009. 89, 225.

## CHAPTER 7. DAYS OF RAGE: BURN, BABY, BURN!

1. "Watts Rebellion (Los Angeles, 1965)." *Martin Luther King Jr. and the Global Freedom Struggle*. Martin Luther King Jr. Research and Education Institute, n.d. Web. 23 Apr. 2013.

2. George Breitman, ed. *Malcolm X Speaks: Selected Speeches and Statements*. London: Secker, 1966. *Google Book Search*. Web. 23 Apr. 2013.

3. Sanford Wexler. *The Civil Rights Movement: An Eyewitness History*. New York: Checkmark, 1998. Print. 245.

4. Michael L. Levine. *African Americans and Civil Rights: From 1619 to the Present*. Phoenix, AZ: Oryx, 1996. Print. 201.

5. Ibid.

6. Sanford Wexler. *The Civil Rights Movement: An Eyewitness History*. New York: Checkmark, 1998. Print. 250.

7. "Coretta Scott King (Obituary)." *Telegraph*. Telegraph Media Group, 1 Feb. 2006. Web. 23 Apr. 2013.

## CHAPTER 8. CIVIL RIGHTS BEYOND THE 1960S

1. Peter B. Levy, ed. *Let Freedom Ring: A Documentary History of the Modern Civil Rights Movement*. New York: Praeger, 1992. Print. 94.

2. "Black Manifesto: The Black National Economic Conference." *New York Review of Books*. NYREV, 10 July 1969. Web. 23 Apr. 2013.

3. Darlene Clark Hine, William C. Hine, and Stanley Harrold. *The African-American Odyssey*. 2nd ed. Upper Saddle River, NJ: Prentice Hall, 2002. Print. 578–579.

4. Ibid.

5. Ibid.

6. Ibid.

7. Joslyn Pine, ed. *Book of African-American Quotations*. Mineola, NY: Dover, 2011. *Google Book Search*. Web. 23 Apr. 2013.

8. "School Desegregation." *Encyclopedia.com*. HighBeam Research-Gale Group, 2005. Web. 24 Apr. 2013.

9. Ibid.

10. Angela Davis. "Masked Racism: Reflections on the Prison Industrial Complex," *ColorLines*. ARC/Colorlines.com, 10 Sep. 1998. Web. 23 Apr. 2013.

11. Michelle Alexander. *The New Jim Crow: Mass Incarceration in the Age of Colorblindness*. New York: New Press, 2010. Print. 14.

12. Ibid.

13. Darlene Clark Hine, William C. Hine, and Stanley Harrold. *The African-American Odyssey*. 2nd ed. Upper Saddle River, NJ: Prentice Hall, 2002. Print. 587–588.

14. "Barack Obama: 2004 Democratic National Convention Keynote Address." *American Rhetoric Online Speech Bank*. American Rhetoric, 27 July 2004. Web. 23 Apr. 2013.

15. Maureen Dowd. "More Phony Myths." *New York Times*. New York Times, 25 June 2008. Web. 23 Apr. 2013.

16. Josephine Hearn, "Black Lawmakers Emotional About Obama's Success." *Politico*. Capitol News Company, 4 June 2008. Web. 23 Apr. 2013.

# INDEX

## ABOUT THE AUTHOR

Michael Capek is a former teacher and author of award-winning nonfiction for young readers, including *Murals: Cave, Cathedral, to Street* and *Artistic Trickery.* His most recent books include *Easter Island, Emperor Qin's Terra Cotta Army,* and *The Steamboat Shuffle*, a historical novel set in 1920s Cincinnati. Michael hopes to explore his roots in the Czech Republic one day soon.

## ABOUT THE CONSULTANT

Steven F. Lawson is professor emeritus of history at Rutgers University in New Jersey. He has a PhD from Columbia University and has taught at the University of South Florida and the University of North Carolina, Greensboro. Lawson's scholarly work centers on the civil rights movement, with extensive focus on black voting rights and politics. In addition to teaching, Lawson has published several books on the subjects of civil rights and black disenfranchisement, including *Running for Freedom: Civil Rights and Black Politics in America Since 1941* and *Debating the Civil Rights Movement.*